Items should be returned on or before the last date shown below. Items not already requested by other borrowers may be renewed in person, in writing or by telephone. To renew, please quote the number on the barcode label. To renew online a PIN is required. This can be requested at your local library.
Renew online @ **www.dublincitypubliclibraries.ie**
Fines charged for overdue items will include postage incurred in recovery. Damage to or loss of items will be charged to the borrower.

**Leabharlanna Poiblí Chathair Bhaile Átha Cliath
Dublin City Public Libraries**

Dublin City
Baile Átha Cliath

Terenure Branch Tel: 4907035

Date Due	Date Due	Date Due
07.		
06. JUL 11.		
- 7 SEP 2018		

D1340267

BLACK MOON

BLACK MOON

Matthew Sweeney

CAPE POETRY

Published by Jonathan Cape 2007

4 6 8 10 9 7 5 3

First published in Great Britain in 2007 by
Jonathan Cape
Random House, 20 Vauxhall Bridge Road,
London SW1V 2SA

www.randomhouse.co.uk

Addresses for companies within The Random House Group Limited can be found at:
www.randomhouse.co.uk

The Random House Group Limited Reg. No. 954009

A CIP catalogue record for this book is available from the British Library

ISBN 9780224080927

The Random House Group Limited makes every effort to ensure that the papers used
in its books are made from trees that have been legally sourced from well-managed
and credibly certified forests. Our paper procurement policy can be found at:
www.randomhouse.co.uk/paper.htm

Typeset by Palimpsest Book Production Limited, Grangemouth, Stirlingshire
Printed and bound in Great Britain by William Clowes Ltd, Beccles, Suffolk

Sing, women o' the Earth,
Sing doun the mune.
When a' the seas are motionless,
Then she will droon.

Helen Adam

CONTENTS

ACKNOWLEDGEMENTS

Aquarius, Atlas, Best of Irish Poetry 2006, Bordercrossing, London Magazine, London Review of Books, Magma, New Yorker, Poetry London, Poetry Review, Poetry Wales, Saw, Southern Review, Southword, The Times Literary Supplement, The Wolf

'Blue' was commissioned by Barbican Education, as part of one of their projects.

I'd like to acknowledge the DAAD's Invited Artist's programme for a year's stipendium in Berlin; also the Santa Maddalena Foundation in Tuscany.

THE RACE

Stavros blows the whistle,
the race is on –
the one-legged monkey
going like a piston
takes an early lead,
but watch that goose,
webbed feet flailing
beak pecking blood,
or over on the right,
the galloping donkey
with the blindfold on –
or surging through the middle
the snorting boar
with the cat on his back,
and at his shoulder,
the charging bear
with fluorescent fur,
but ostrich, the favourite
is limping to a halt,
and the leopard lies dead,
face in the dirt,
and the rabbit is hiding
in a palm tree.
And standing at the start,
howling his head off,
is the tied-up wolf.

THE MISSION

Hiding in the wolfhound's kennel,
hoping the big brute won't return,
he takes the tiny photo out again.
Such a pretty face to make a hole in,
such sad eyes without a reason –
yet . . . Unless she's always known,
the way dogs know, and disappear
deep into the woods to die alone.
If only she would do the same.
He turns the photo upside down
till her nose sticks up in the U
of her hair, and beneath it
the place he must focus on.
Righted again, there's less of a smile
on those lips, but still a ghost of one.
The face is the face of a battler –
he hopes she's not a gun woman.
He hopes her hound won't save her
by tearing off his face. At that
he hears a car crunch over pebbles.
He replaces the photo in his wallet,
frees his revolver from its holster,
inches his way to the cold air,
whispering her name over and over.

THE DOORS

Behind the door was another door
and behind that was another.

The first door was black, as befitted
a four-storey Georgian house
on a street shaded by oaks.

The second door was the grey
of the sky before rain.

The third door was blue, or blue-
green — let's say cobalt — with a stiff
black wrought-iron handle

which took the shape of a mermaid
instead of a dog or a dragon.

Or the rattlesnake I expected
to rear up, hissing, at me
when I crossed the threshold.

No chime announced me.
No animal or person met me.

The corridor I looked down
was lined with male portraits.
The rugs had embroidered females.

The ghost of incense haunted
the air I hardly breathed.

I took a couple of half-steps
then stood there, listening.
I heard the portraits breathing

and from some distant room
a cuckoo clock cuckooing.

My smile turned into a cough
that echoed off the walls
and infiltrated the house.

The women on the first rug
were grinning at me.

All the eyes in the portraits
were turned my way.
I looked back at the door

heard the lock click, then beyond
another lock, then another.

NO SUGAR

Sitting, upright, on the sofa,
sandwiched between a pair of twins,
both blond, both beautiful,
wearing the same red leather
miniskirts, the same faces,
the same green sparkling eyes,
I find myself thinking of melon,
green-fleshed, cool from the fridge,
sliced cross ways in half,
the seeds scooped out, the hole
filled with chilled Sauternes.
A cough emanating from one twin
is echoed by the other. I chuckle,
they chuckle in stereo, and outside
the streetlight comes on, a dog
howls, a car alarm starts to blare,
while in this white-carpeted room
the newly-permed mother arrives
with a silver tray, on which sit
three delicate china cups, each with
its leaf-patterned saucer, a tea pot
escaped from Shanghai, a jug
with a peacock on it and milk
of some kind inside. But no sugar,
not a single solitary grain.

INSOMNIA

Everywhere it's raining except here
where the mosquitoes thrive
and the car alarms wail at each other
all through the dog-moaning night,
and just before dawn that smell
of onions frying brings the image
of a fat ghost chef whose insomnia
is dealt with like this, making me
rush to the kitchen to catch him
but he and the smell are always gone.
And sleep has no chance at all then,
so rather than ride the toss-&-turning
horse I go naked onto the balcony
to count the lights left on in the flats,
trying to imagine who is up early
and who is late to bed, and soon
the night train will arrive from the north
to rest and be fed, the woken crows
will start the feral cats, and I will add
my wolf howl, then wait for the shouts.

THE SWEATMARK

The sweatmark on his T-shirt that day
made a map of Ireland, not the map
you'd see in a current atlas, but one
like the ur-map that hung on his wall
at home — where it never got this hot,
not in a hundred years. He wiped
his leaking brow with his half-sleeve
and held the base of the T-shirt out
to look at the sweatmark again.
It was Ireland, all right, even seen
upside down. His own county,
Donegal, was over his right nipple.
Kerry kicked towards the liver
while Dublin was nowhere at all.
He sleeked down his warm hair
with his fingers. What did this mean,
if anything? He got sweatmarks
all these days, but never a map before.
Was it a signal calling him back?
Why else was the T-shirt only marked
in that spot, unlike every other time?
He wondered should he phone home.
Then that voice in his head he hated
told him to take the T-shirt off
and shove it in the laundry basket.
If it really was a map and a sign
it would survive the launderette —
which it didn't, not that that proved
anything, he afterwards thought.
But that sweatmark never reappeared.

AIR SHOW

High over the tower block
the helicopter hovered,
with a white rope ladder
twirling beneath it
and on it, a man
in a red tracksuit
held out the Soviet flag.
Then the Internationale
blared from a speaker
with the man joining in.
People were arriving
on the roof, and one man
clapped loudly, and cheered
while another booed.
When the song ended
the dangling man bowed
and waved the flag
in an arc from side to side,
before sending it sailing
through the blue of the sky,
while he clambered up
and into the helicopter
which buzzed in a circle,
then took off for the east.

THE SNOWY OWL

Over the heads of the firing squad
flew a snowy owl, who oohooed twice
just before they pulled their triggers
and as the woman slumped on her ropes,
blood splattering her white dress,
the owl landed on her shoulder,
oohooed again, and swivelled its big-
eyed gaze over all the uniformed men,
one of whom raised his rifle
but the captain knocked it away
while the owl pecked at some blood
on the woman's breast, smearing
its own breast feathers, then glared,
it seemed, at the transfixed men,
before swooping off, barely missing
the head of one, making them all
turn to watch it glide away, and hear
one more oohoo echo through the sky.

EXCAVATION

Somewhere in these woods a crashed plane
is buried in undergrowth, the wings
broken off, black crosses still visible
to anyone who'd hack down to see them,
and if this person were then to excavate
the crushed cockpit, liberate the broken
skeleton, prop it up against a pine tree,
a low humming would be heard above
the flies and bees, a humming that took on
German, that danced about on the wind
while the tail, with its black crosses,
was dug out of roots, grass, fallen branches
as gunfire once again filled these hills
after sixty years, and shells and tracer
flew overhead, but no tree would be hit,
nor would fires whoosh through leaves
to the delight of the fool in the hill castle
out with his grappa on the rooftop,
Marlene blaring through the speakers
singing to the crashed pilot in the woods.

SLEEP

Alongside the blown-up tank,
wearing a too-big, bloodstained uniform
sleeps the boy. His hair is long,
his face and hands are filthy.
He is clutching the top half
of a rifle. Beyond his feet
a feral dog lies, watching him.
Around him is rubbled wasteland,
no house intact. Was one of them
his home? No matter now.
Ahead, the forest is on fire.
Shots echo above the car-wrecks,
but no snipers can be seen.
That crow on the tank's useless gun
is the lookout. The boy sleeps on.
Whimpering, the dog inches nearer.
The drone of a plane gets louder
till the air fills with pages
fluttering to the ground, covering
the boy who turns onto his back
and snores. The crow flaps aloft,
making the dog bark, till a hand
grabs a stone and throws it,
all with eyes closed. Then he's up
on his feet, the rifle stump
swivelling every way, his eyes
catching everything. He bends,
picks up a page, tries to read it,
shouts out, crumples it into a ball,
sends it hurling back at the sky.

THE SOLDIERS

Send the soldiers in, *mein Kamerad*.
That immigrant den needs cleaning up.
Take the males out and shoot them.
Blindfold all the women, cram them
into a van that'll burn rubber
all the way to that house on Wannsee,
push them in and lock the door.

Is it *Meissner Wein* you'll want later?
I'll order a crate and chill it.
I'll ask Lotte and Sabine to dress
accordingly, and ease up on the lipstick.
That flautist from Dresden can play
the Mozart suites you like so well.
And, of course, I'll cook for you –

no meat, needless to say, not today.
I suggest pasta with king prawns first,
then *Dorade*, served with *Pfifferlinge*,
and finally, a lemon-and-lime sorbet.
You'll have a shower before we sit down –
the soap, you'll notice, smells of melon.
Your favourite suit will be waiting for you.

This city was half ruined twice, in
different ways, and it mustn't be again.
You owe this to your grandchildren.
Remember the times Berlin was German.
I'll make suggestions to the Chancellor.
Clasp hands with me and hug, *Kamerad*.
Your name is about to enrich stone.

NAKED

Take off your shoes, he said,
    and hurl them into the sea.
Take off that satin shirt
    and hand it to me,
and it had better fit, he said,
    or you're fucking dead.
Take off those grey cords
    and hope you're my size.
Take off the underpants
    and pull them over your eyes,
and blind, take off each sock
    while waggling your cock,
ignoring the laughs I gift you
    in this ghastly hour —
for *you*, that is, he said
    before laughing some more
and slapping me on the rump
    commanding me to jump,
Higher! Higher! he shouted
    and I heard a gun click
as sweat bubbled out of me
    and I began to get sick.
Stop that or I fucking shoot!
    You disgusting brute!
He kicked me in the balls
    till I doubled up.
Stand up straight! he roared.
    You contemptible pup!
And he hit me on the head
    with the gun till I bled.
More mess! he bellowed.
    You're worse than a pig.
Then he handed me a spade
    and ordered me to dig.

PRIMETIME

The ambushed US soldier
took three of them with him
before they got his head off,
and this they put in a bag
to bring back to the capital
where they washed it,
combed the blond hair,
placed it on red velvet
on a round silver tray
which they spotlit,
pointed a TV camera at,
and the leading ventriloquist,
fluent in American
after a year at Stanford,
spoke from the head,
saying 'I have a message
for holiday-king, Bush'
(and at that, somehow,
the eyes sprang open,
and the stare came close-up)
'We need a holiday from here,
all of us, right now.'
The eyes closed again.
The lips bent in a sort-of smile
that led in the drumming,
first low, then, loud, louder
and ventriloquised laughter
came from the head,
which was rocking,
then all went fuzzy and faded
till reprieved and replayed
over and over at primetime.

THE LETTER

When the pristine snow turned yellow,
then the wind blew down half the trees
I knew to take the next plane out –
I flew to Durban, rented a loft,
bought a TV, simply to watch the news,
and yes, barely a week later, the earth-
quake struck, reducing Berlin to rubble.
I saw, fleetingly, the remains of my flat
with alsatian dogs running through it.
It's then I sat down to my letter –
to God the only. I bollocked Him
for so much destruction in one city –
why didn't He pick Zurich, or somewhere?
Did He know how much I'd enjoyed
my six months' residence in Friedrichshain,
how I'd finally felt at home in a place?
I told Him about the red walls of the study,
about the way the early morning sun crept in
and lit up the kitchen. I explained that
a dissident *Ossie* architect had designed it.
I asked Him if He'd like a ruined Heaven.
I accused Him of being the ur-Nazi,
said I'd never venture inside a church again.
Then, not knowing God's secret address,
I threw my letter into the open fire,
certain that, as it carboned to ash,
it would rise all the way to Heaven.
I'd learned that from an angel, no less.

SIGNATURE

'Sign the document!' he shouted,
shoving me to the table
where a printed form was lying
but what those words meant
was as lost to me as peace.

'Sign there!' he hissed,
jabbing with his finger
at a space beside a colon,
behind which words queued
in a language I couldn't tell.

'Sign the thing, damn you,
or I'll blow your head off!'
and he parted the hairs
on the back of my neck
with the muzzle of his gun.

Then he burst into laughter
and clouds of beery breath
enveloped my face.
'You don't know, do you?
Haven't a clue what it is!'

'Give me your scrawl, anyway.
What you don't know
won't kill you but I will
if you don't sign, so what
do you have to lose, eh?'

And he picked up the pen
and forced it into my hand
while pressing the gun
hard against my lower skull.
And the clock ticked on.

CAPTURED

Punching and kicking the tall man
    who held her off the ground,
she kept her eyes on the fat man
    who made no sound, just sat there
in the yellow chair under the African drum
    staring at her, not smiling at her,
as the tall man carried her to him,
    dumped her on the lion carpet,
withdrew to the rocking chair, while a fat
    foot settled on a blond head
gently, for at most, a minute,
    then withdrew, and a pudgy finger
wiped away two tears and squeezed
    a nose before two plump hands
crashed together, so the tall man rose, eased
    her to her feet, led her out through
the carved mahogany doorframe, past the stone
    vulture, the stained wood leopard,
all of them and her lit by a moon
    that the glass made yellow, sick, cold,
while behind her, the shuffling feet,
    the gasped-out breath of the fat man
powered her forward to whatever she'd meet.

THE FIRE

The fire was chasing me
so I ran, stopping only to
try each door I reached
but all of them were locked,
their windows kept inside.
And on the doors, the Russians –
Lenin, Stalin, Khrushchev,
Andropov – glared at me,
as the fire roared and hissed.
I could smell the air of hell,
and myself roasting. I ran,
stopping at Gorbachev
whom I threw myself at.
He smiled on. I tried again.
Nothing, a dislocated shoulder.
The fire was at my arse,
so I galloped on, past Yeltsin,
past Putin, shouting now,
as if anyone could hear me,
as if anyone would care.

THE SCREAM

He went on deck in a hurricane
because he heard the scream —
the choral scream of those he'd killed —
he heard it above the wind and rain,
above the clinking of glasses of rum,
the drunken laughter and talk of women,
the smell of cabbage and boiled ham,
the wobbly songs of the Captain.
He heard the scream grow louder
till his skull began to cave in,
so he ran out, and onto a deck
which tossed him against the rail
that he climbed up and jumped from,
down through the scream-filled wind.

THE HUNGER ARTIST AT HOME

After Kafka

In the days following my fastings
I sit in my empty cage, the door open,
hearing again the taunts of the crowds
who poke me, accuse me of stashed food,
curse me when I don't respond.
What do they know, the imbeciles?
I would gladly double my forty days
if they'd let me. Then I might
approach the state of skin-covered bone
I aspire to, see in the night –
become a creature as light as the things
I surround myself with: the melon gourd,
the empty ostrich egg, the crow's skull.
They cannot imagine this, the fools.
I nibble my foul-tasting crusts,
reach out a hand to set spinning
the globe of the moon, close my eyes
to imagine a skeleton slowly walking
across the moon's surface, then climbing
into a crater to lie there and be still.

UNDERGROUND

He lived in a hole in the ground,
down a ladder, in the bottom room.

This was large but low-ceilinged.
Wooden beams kept the earth up,
rugs were draped on the caked walls

apart from the one with the fresco
he'd done the winter of the shootings.

The other rooms were mostly empty
though sometimes strangers stayed –
then he'd know to remain underground.

When he went out it was usually night –
he hunted with the owls, the foxes.

He'd go to the spring in the forest,
fill two five-litre bottles.
He'd find mushrooms at first light.

He fussed over his homemade wine –
favoured chestnut and elm-root.

Sometimes a badger straying
across his concealed roof
would hear the music he played.

Once a mole came to visit him.
He captured it, forced it to be his pet.

He wrote and read by lamplight –
writing in the morning,
reading all through the night.

He wrote about the terror campaign.
He read about easier times.

Long ago he'd lived with a woman –
in a high windy flat,
with different glimpses of the sea.

When sleep came, and it was seldom,
he'd often dream of this

and he'd wake, saying her name.
It was well she wasn't living here
in this country, these times.

It was well she wasn't down with him
in this hole in the ground.

SAMARKAND

The magazine featured his story
beneath a nude author's photo.

The story was full of severed hands
sticking up out of snow,

and a gay cop with a white cat
unpicking the conundrum.

In the photo the bottom hair was blond,
the scant top hair was black.

The sky-blue eyes were half-closed.
The smile was as thin as a new moon.

The magazine had a large circulation
among the medical fraternity.

On the cover of this issue was a worm
emerging from a woman's ear.

Not all newsagents stocked it.
The financier was an ex-astronaut

who'd vetoed the original title, *Fog*,
settling instead for *Samarkand*.

Every item in that first issue
contained some reference to sand.

HIDING

Somewhere in Kreuzberg a man
hides from the Sultan of Sleep.
He's been hiding for ten years,
moved from tenement to tenement
by bearded boys, and all the while
the Sultan's minions come sniffing,
asking questions in bad Turkish,
worse German, waving Euro notes
at the eyes of curlyhaired kids
who run to their shouting mamas.

No, in Kreuzberg the man is safe
and the Sultan has many would-be
assassins — the one time he came
with three bodyguards, a chunk
of the Wall bloodied his features
and laughter seeped into the sky
mixed with the smell of grilled lamb
that women bring to the hiding man,
together sometimes with wine
that helps him re-tell his story.

STRING

If ever the thought strikes you
to head off for the Arctic,
be sure to take with you
a large roll of string,
for the Inuits up there
can make string tell stories —
anyone who's a poet
is also a string-artist
and talks to the kids as well.
So you'd better practise
before you get there.
Read up on your history, too —
that fellow, Lord Franklin,
who disappeared; whose wife
liked to swing in a hammock
and who offered all kinds
of rewards for anyone
who could bring the body
back from the ice. If he'd
taken a big enough roll
of string, and trailed it
behind him all the cold way,
she could have wrapped up
and found him herself.
And even today an Inuit
string-artist tells that story
to hordes of visitors
without uttering a word.

THE THING

The thing is we don't know a thing
about the thing that's going on
over there, in thingamabob's hideout
where he's holed up with thingy,
the one in the red thingamajig –
and that thing with Swiss number plates
they landed here in, nothing
less roadworthy ever crossed a border –
the police should have a thing or two
to say about it – about this whole thing
we can't tell you anything about,
what we know is one thing inevitably
leads to another, and nothing would
surprise us less than to hear a gunshot,
and as things stand we wouldn't
be able to do a single thing about it.

COMING HOME

He crossed the sea in a coracle
to show it could be done.

The coracle was made of pigskins
stretched over pig bones

and held most of the rest of the pig
in stews, salamis, and hams.

He had a paddle, a sail, a motor
and a bottle of Talisker,

a Walkman primed with Latin jazz,
a translation of the *Inferno*,

a photo of a topless woman,
a lifebelt, a flare-gun, a revolver.

On his head he wore a headdress
of green parrot feathers

and on his body was a wetsuit
under an Afghan coat.

As he approached the Irish coast
he flew the tricolour

and as he veered for the pier
he stood up and saluted

the statue at the harbour mouth,
while whistling 'The Soldier's Song'.

This earned him a few shouts
from a staggering drunk

and cheering and clapping
from a gang of smoking girls.

He bowed, lassoed the capstan,
and hauled himself onto Ireland.

BEING MET

Two cars arrived at the airport,
both of them to collect Cecil.
The two drivers stood on the concourse
outside the exit from customs,
each holding up Cecil's name.
His bag was last on the carousel,
so when the glass door released him
only these two were waiting.
He went up to one, then the other.
He left his bag on the ground.
The two were trying to persuade him
that they were the embassy driver.
They began haranguing each other
to drive off in an empty car.
Cecil heard a song in his head
but the words were forgotten.
He felt like the rope in a tug of war.
He wanted to grab his bag and run
but each of them had it by the handle
and neither was letting go.

THE PATH

Finding the path was easy
but following it into the sun
with no shades on, or no bend
to give the eyes respite . . .
Not even the trees helped,
lined, as they were, on both sides,
and the promised glint of sunlight
sparkling on the water . . .
Well, whose promise was it?
Glynn's! And the stories he told
of a beach of white sand,
around it, a horseshoe of hills
and between them the bluest water
in the middle of which, not deep
lay a sunken boat. All this
combated the sun, and those flies
it sent to drink the sweat
that bubbled out of his face . . .
And water, why had he brought none?
He changed the hand at his eyes,
lengthened his stride a little
while keeping rhythm, searched ahead
and seeing no change of light, switched
to the sky in the hope of gulls.

BORDERS

for Dennis O'Driscoll

I have seen the Ukraine, across a river,
but not been there, not yet.
I have crossed a bridge, on foot,
into Poland, spent fifteen minutes.
My passport says I'm still there.
I have criss-crossed the border
at Geneva, leaving me dizzy.
I was held for half an hour
at the East German *Zoll*, arguing
that I was the passport photo.
I've sat in the train for hours
in the no-man's-land that links
Hungary and Romania. I've come
within 10 kilometres of Bulgaria.
I have stood at the customs in Basel
with a scribbled sign for Dublin.
I've walked round Berwick in the fog
hearing Scottish accents in English mouths.
I decided I needed to be born
as my mother approached the Irish border.

GETTING THERE

The signpost said 10 kilometres
but looking at the map I doubted it,
the rain showed no sign of stopping
and the car was leaking, and night,
big blanket night was closing in.

I looked out at the dripping trees,
at the not so distant mountains
whose peaks were gone, and I
wished for a small rogue sun
to zoom here from another planet.

Might as well wish for banknotes
to flutter down. The windscreen-
wipers toiled away, shoving streams
left and right, making a noise
that called up a clapped-out pump.

Suddenly a soaked hitchhiker
jumped out from behind a tree,
his long hair straggly conduits
for the rain, but splashing him,
ignoring him, we drove on.

I thought of that tightrope walker
I'd seen fall into the Thames
to be fished out by the River Police.
In the wing mirror, the hitchhiker
waved a fist and I looked away.

I concentrated on the road ahead,
on the pothole puddles, and then,
after a bend round a crag, we saw
just there, in front of us, the hotel.
We sat on in the car to make sure.

THE CURE

Fighting off a cold, he rode his bike
down the road to the sea
where a wind blew in from Greenland
holding the gulls back in flight,
flinging litter around, creating waves
surfers exchanged emails about –
and yes, they were represented here,
a couple standing by the open boot
of their car, donning black wetsuits,
then running with their surfboards
into that teeming, frothing ocean.
For a while he watched them falling
off, climbing on again, all the time
whooping and laughing, and thought:
What gives me kicks like that?
Reading? Not likely! Sex? Long ago.
Food? Once in a green moon!
Alcohol? Only when celebrating,
and when have I last done this?
A gust flung his hair over his face,
making him shiver, and a coughing fit
encouraged him onto the bike again
which he laboured with uphill
but only as far as the new hotel
where the bar was quiet at this time,
and the barman with the moustache
knew all about colds, and the way
a hot whiskey quickly disabled them.

THE ASCENT

Halfway up the mountain, he stopped
to let his breath catch up, and his eyes
took in the calm sea, with beyond it,
in a haze, what had to be Scotland.

No boat or ship interrupted the blue
that had swallowed the sky – water
so cold, even in summer, that no one
stayed in long without a wetsuit.

He swigged some warmer water
from the bottle on his belt, coughing
as he replaced the cap, and set
his booted feet climbing again.

He had no flag with him to stick
in the summit, if he could call it that,
but he did have a purple towel
he would drape over the cairn there.

He'd make sure it would stay put
for weeks at least, so they'd talk
in the bars about it, coming outside
in daylight to stand and point up at it.

He would say nothing, if asked.
He dried his face with the towel
and gauged he was about halfway.
It would flatten out a bit now.

Twenty years ago he remembered
half-running to the top from here
then standing there, waving his arms
and yelling, as if anyone cared.

Today he'd take his time to arrive,
and once there, he'd smooth the towel
over the stones, with one or two on top,
and he wouldn't look down at all.

INHERITANCE

Standing on the hilltop,
he could see the island –
could make out clearly
the old family cottage
not that he'd ever slept
or boiled a kettle in it
but he'd heard stories,
seen one yellow photograph,
and now it was his. A roof
of sorts was there but no
front wall, and the gable
on the sea side was air.
At least a road passed it,
potholed, no doubt,
but bumpable over,
and the pier looked intact.
He'd have local masons
out there before the week
was over, then builders,
roofers, carpenters.
He'd buy himself a boat.
He'd dig out records
of life on the island,
ended fifty years before.
He'd have a helicopter
airlift a generator,
then a cooker, a fridge,
a freezer, and wine,
cases of it, with the food
to go with it, though fish
might be caught, and rabbits
must thrive there. In time
he'd try a herb garden . . .

But now it was the hotel
and dinner — roast lamb,
he'd noticed. And after,
a cognac with the manager
who'd known his father.

ANOTHER COUNTRY

for Thomas Lynch

And then, finally, we'd found them,
the dolphins, and circled among them
till one leapt through the air, turning,
before diving beneath the boat,
and after they'd wave-swum away
we spied a solitary porpoise,
keeping its distance, as it would;
then, led by low-flying shearwaters,
we churned in close to the cliff
where fulmars rode the wind
above a standing line of cormorants,
behind which, on a grassy ledge,
a pair of curly-horned puck goats
lay, soaking up the sun;
then there was the mother seal
watching from the submerged cave
till, increasing speed, we chugged away
and, guided by youngster gulls,
we made for the pier and the border.

VANESSA ATALANTA

Already November, and the last red admiral
is flapping around the light. Its mate
sits dead, wings folded, in the bottom corner
of the window. No poking will resurrect it.
Above it a bee, almost dead, clings to the glass.
The flier pirouettes in the hot air, flashing open
its red and white frescoes, then closing to
the black wings that mimic its dead brother,
above whom the bee, in a last campaign, moves
stiffly across the glass, too tired for flight,
hanging on, now that the heating's activated,
which might give Vanessa Atalanta another
day to open and close its gaudy lungs,
dance figures of eight in the air, a diminutive
Italian Richthofen, showing off to itself
and to the light it lands on, but never
for long, until it's dried and baked there.

PROCESSION

for Christopher North

He pushed the wheelchair up the hill
to the old church that opened once a year
for the arrival of the Easter procession
fresh from the winding path and the stations,
each with its defaced Roman soldiers.

His octogenarian father looked down
at the terraces other Roman soldiers
had set out for vines – long supplanted
by fig and olive trees, though rumours
of vine-revival echoed round the valley.

Up above, the mountains formed a line,
a barrier between them and the sea.
His father asked to be helped up to peer
through a window at the small altar,
at the icons, the all-but-unused pews.

Going down, the problem wasn't straining,
or sweating, but braking. They made it to Pepe's
bar in the Square, by the newer church
with its bells and Rwandan padre who stood
at the door as he arrived at the outside table

with a tray holding a bottle of red *El Coto
Rioja*, two glasses, a plate of *chorizo*,
to find his father rapt in an older man's
struggle uphill with a Zimmer frame, then turning,
taking wine, to toast the man, who didn't notice.

NOCTURNE

Take me by Easyjet to Venice,
hijack a gondola at night,
pole me out in the moonlight
to the centre of the lagoon,
sit there, light up a cigar,
swig from your hipflask,
while I sketch the island church
of San Giorgio Maggiore
again and again, until I say
take me back to my easel,
pole as fast as you can,
and I'm looking back at the dark
silhouette, and the dots of light
on the grey-green water,
whistling a nocturne, smiling
as I see hanging before me
the finished watercolour –
I may even add an etching
which I'll give to you, but not
the painting. That's for Anu.

THE SANDAL

Among the debris was a sandal,
a pale blue Italian exile
useless without its twin, we thought,
but she, being Sicilian, grabbed it,
mounted it on black card,
sprayed it with silver droplets,
glued an anchovy skeleton beneath it,
and above it, a dried scorpion,
sprinkled it with sea water,
said two dialect prayers,
danced with an invisible partner
while singing a madrigal,
held the sandal up and kissed it
then hurled it at the full moon.

BLUE

When I saw Yves Klein's women
naked except for blue paint
I remembered the silver man
in Berlin, at the Brandenburg Gate
so I tracked down Klein's blue,
filled a bucket with it,
took every stitch of clothes off,
painted myself all over – *every*
bit of me, not like those women!
And when the paint was dry
I hopped on the 73 bus,
bumped my way to Big Ben
where I bluely disembarked
to stand, assaulted by flashbulbs,
outside the Houses of Parliament,
not moving, or even twitching,
but humming one note on and on.

HOW TO WIN THE LOTTERY

Stick some gum on the wall,
press a pound coin into that
then bow to it, backing away
till you negotiate the door
and end up in the corridor,
concentrating with all your might
on that ersatz gold circle,
thought-sucking it out to you,
making it fall to the floor
and roll after you out the door
to stop inches from your feet
whereupon you pick it up
and reward it with a kiss,
then reach for pen and paper
to jot down six numbers
that tumble out at random
while you're rubbing the coin,
six digits shook from a dream
where the deeds of an island
are about to acquire your name.

REGGAE

Humming a reggae song, he bopped
along the road, doffing his rainbow hat
to a pair of ancient chatting ladies
who stared at his hair, tut-tutting.
A fire-engine swung round the corner,
siren blaring, so he hopped aside
to let it roar past, causing a mongrel
to howl as if the Devil himself
was scorching by on a motorbike.
Above him a blue zeppelin floated,
advertising itself across the sky.
A nod and a grin went the way
of the boy fixing a puncture
on the pavement. He clicked
his fingers and hummed louder
bending and rising to the rhythm,
as three seagulls swooped down
to fight over a dropped ice-cream,
causing him to cackle, till one
pecked at his boot, and a kick
sent it flying towards the sun.
He sashayed on, through the feathers,
catching a couple, and laughing,
never missing the reggae beat.

PARTY

The firework went off in the box
causing screams and laughter –
and a knocked-over bottle of wine,
then someone put on The Doors
up so loud the panes vibrated
while a tipsy blonde sang along.

That was when the cat freaked out –
Wallace had slipped her acid
stirred into chopped-up rabbit.
She spun round like a compass needle
at the Pole, then dropped dead.
The identical Finnish twins shrieked.

No one was guarding the telephone,
so when the wah-wahs sounded,
and a head out the window reported
the cops were here, I assumed
the flushing of the West Cork grass,
while Wallace hid the corpse.

What a waste, I thought, as the two
cops – a man and a woman – made
the most perfunctory search, he
laughing, saying the grass smelt good,
she tight-lipped but elsewhere.
Wallace, I think, showed them out.

WHAT SIZE?

'What size of shoes has he?'
   asked the unrecognised voice
through the labyrinth of the phone,
   and the receiver was held
away from the head but not put down,
   nor did any answer come.
'What size of shoes has he?'
   came from that plastic again,
but the siren of a passing fire-engine
   was all that went in,
then the ringing of a church bell
   and a chorus of dog-howls,
and afterwards that steady breathing
   that permitted no words,
so a musical whistling began,
   first soft, then louder,
dancing out of the phone, before
   stopping, abruptly, on a high
note to let in that voice again –
   'Tell him I've got them for him,
they'll be delivered soon' –
   then silence became dialling tone.

BLACK

Unlike other times, there was no warning.
The meteorologists all stayed mum.
No one flew halfway across the planet
with camcorders at the ready. And oddly,
this time — although just as slow-happening
as before — the moon didn't cross the sun,
but the latter's light gradually went out
and it never came back on again.

We didn't know this till later, of course.
By their wailing the dogs and cats did,
but we didn't see, though a few evangelists
(who grew as the day went on) took to howling
prayers at the switched-off sky, and cars
drove slowly with voices coming loud
through speakers telling us not to panic,
that God would return us our sun.

At former nightfall time we got our moon,
and luckily it was near full. Many voices
were raised to it, though some questioned
how it had light without the sun. The Devil
was mentioned, and people crossed themselves.
Others drew coats around shivering bodies,
shouting out hymns, while the pubs
did the best business they'd ever done.

That didn't last. Most folk took to their homes,
never coming out, except for shopping trips
that soon became desperate as supplies dwindled
until wizened potatoes were fought over,
onions thrown. Extra streetlights and patio
heaters couldn't coax any out except the young
who had the bars to themselves, though offies
did record business, and pizza bakers thrived.

After one month of darkness, when the looting
had been crushed, the suicides started to happen
and very quickly a pattern set in – hangings
from lampposts, with the light full on.
Curiously, the police took no notice of this
beyond cutting the corpses down. Only kids
too young to know anything else would cope:
rat-hunters, blood-drinkers, ignorant of the sun.

ASSASSIN

Before the dog barked
he'd killed it – piano wire,
wristwork. The glass
in the door lost a circle,
a gloved hand snaked in,
the door opened without a key.

The cat knew to be silent.
The parrot said nothing
when a coat draped its cage.
He swallowed a cough,
noticed the Goya etching,
smiled, and climbed the stairs.

The almost-full moon stared
through a landing window.
He smelled faint eucalyptus,
heard a clock strike two,
checked, absurdly, that his shirt
was buttoned, climbed on.

His hand held the doorknob
for a minute before turning.
She was there in the bed,
gently snoring. He took out
the Nazi dagger, plunged it
once, wiped it on the duvet, left.

MOSCOW

Wearing a home-made bandana
of an East German flag,
accompanied by a dog in a frayed leather coat,
she walked into the travel agent
and asked for an air-ticket to Moscow.

'Just one?' the blond boy asked,
looking over the counter at the dog
who growled a greeting,
then lay down and breathed so heavily
each breath was a snore.

'Did I ask for one, or not?'
the woman muttered. She wasn't
the type you'd abandon in church,
or give a horse to at Christmas.
The boy fiddled with his computer.

He asked her when she was thinking of.
'Today', she said. 'Yesterday,
if you could manage it.' Outside
a road-drill was chewing a street.
The boy thought of home-time.

He clicked his mouse on Moscow,
but today's flights were full.
'Shall I try for tomorrow?' he asked.
'No good', the woman said, getting up,
oblivious to whether the dog rose too.

NIGHT MUSIC

He stood on the roof with a saxophone
playing across the road. It was dark,
no one could see him. Passing cars —
though few at this hour — drowned him
out, but he swooped back into hearing,
sending high arcs of sound across
to the block of flats on the other side.
A woman stuck her head out a window,
shouting. A man fired potato missiles,
all missing. He played on, now soft as
a rainbow, now firm as a promontory.
A white cat looked up, miaowing.
A boy lay on top of a bunk bed, smiling.
He played to the owls that flitted past.
He played to the cosmonaut on the moon.
He'd never played as sweetly before
and no one was recording this. He tried
one high bright hopscotch between stars,
holding the notes, as if lovemaking.
A light went on in the top flat, left.
A woman stood sleepily on a balcony.
He sent some fluttery notes her way
just as the first reddening of sunlight
hit the sky. Then he was off, soaring
to Mars and back, diving to the bottom
of the Atlantic, as the red deepened, the sun
climbed above the roofs, paling to a white
that blinded him, told him to stop, pack
his sax away, bow once, go to his rope-
ladder, climb down, disappear into the day.

THE SNAKE

He posted her a snake instructed not to bite her.
It came in a long cardboard tube, pricked all over.
It was yellow and black, with red squares and diamonds
to go with the yellow cat, the black terrapin, the red
flowers of the cacti that were the feelers of her flat.
The cat did well to be wary of this cold-blooded slitherer,
this swaying, tongue-waving dancer who followed its
mistress from room to room, as his wriggly ambassador.
She did not know it wouldn't bite her, and winced
when it brushed across her feet but when this happened
regularly, when she woke to find it lying on her body
or coiled around her neck, she began to accept it, want it,
come home early, saying she had to feed her pets.
He posted her a second snake instructed to bite her.

OPERA

Over an espresso and slice of apple cake
he thought of his ending up again
in that hotel near the opera guarded by
two lions with women's faces and breasts —
breasts like hers actually, that he'd uncovered
in possibly that same hotel room,
before accompanying her into the shower
to do things soap was not intended for.
Draining his coffee, and walking back
in a rain as light as mist, he asked
the stone men on the roof of the opera
if they remembered her. One pointed
down to the lion below, and he saw now
it had her face. Of course, she loved
the opera, how could he forget, how
could she not linger here, so he knew
she'd lope up to his room again that night,
and reclaim her woman's body at the door.

FLOATING

He saw her floating in the Danube.
She was face-up, her long hair
streaming like Ophelia's. Behind her
swam two cats, one big, one small.
They would escort her to Romania.
He wanted to dive in and follow them
but he knew he couldn't swim that far.
Instead, he started a high keening
that soon went choral, as folk joined in –
even the cats contributed their wailing.
By now the Danube's banks were crowded.
A boat set off after her, with priests
in the prow, but the engine stalled midstream.
She floated on, the mob moving with her,
him at the head. He took off his hat
and threw it out across the water, but it fell
short and floated there till a dog retrieved it.
He put it back on, dripping, then waved
as the walled banks gave way to brambles
and she floated round a bend out of sight.

PRACTICE

I sailed a boat into a small natural bay,
watched by a penguin welcoming committee.

I fired a rope-trailing harpoon into the ice,
then pulled myself in to a flat place

where I could disembark with my 4 wood.
I teed up and whacked a really good

shot way down the ice, the ball skittering
when it landed, the penguins staring

but not applauding. I teed up another,
and this time half the penguins ran for cover

or would have, if there'd been more than ice.
Others, though, stayed in their space,

gaping, as I struck eight more sweet shots,
then, bowing, I got back into my boat,

untied the rope, yanked out the harpoon,
and aimed the boat at the great ocean.

CURRY

It smelt of curry,
the room smelt of curry,
but how? And why?
No cooker, no spices,
no Indian anywhere
near, no plates, forks,
spoons. But that yellow
there on the wall
was turmeric, and that
pod on the floor
was a cardamom.
Messy eaters, whoever
they were. And yes,
two empty beer bottles
in the bin, and crumbs
or shards of poppadom.
It made him hungry,
hungry for a curry.
They could have left
a portion of dhal,
a spoonful of spinach,
fifty grains of rice –
he could now make out
exactly what they'd had.
But where could he go
to obtain the same
or anything like it –
the airport? So how
had the smell got here?
He sucked it in,
muttering in Irish,
grabbed his red jacket,

vacated the flat
to go to a place where
a pizza came brazen
with chilli and garlic.

THE TOOTHBRUSH SELLER OF MANGALIA

The toothbrush seller of Mangalia
has a red T-shirt on, and a bag on the ground
with samples of various brushes in it,
all of which he claims to be the best, waving
a select handful at the mouths of passers by,
most of whom walk through him,
in their race to the beach, so he dances
on the street, brandishing his cavity-stoppers,
till the next sun-junkie enters his space
and leaves again – but occasionally
one hesitates, holds a toothbrush, even
(women with toddlers are the best here),
then returns it, smiles, and minces off,
making him dance a bit fiercer, swivel
across the street to hop on a half-wall and peer
everyway, let a few chewers pass, unaccosted,
change his samples, re-set his grin, and then,
out of nowhere, a man examines a toothbrush,
nods, buys one for all his family, *four
sales at once!* thinks the toothbrush seller,
for a minute Mr Happy of Mangalia,
but the bag on the ground is still heavy,
so he lightens it very slightly, and waves the
fished-out samples, thinking of that first beer.

SUNRISE ON THE BLACK SEA

She sets her phone alarm for five
to get to the beach in time
to see the sun climb from the sea –

not any sea, mind you, the Black Sea
which is over there in the east,
and she's on the western shore –

perfect, in other words, for catching
a watery sunrise, which she claims
is the only kind worthy of the name –

how, for example, is a sun scaling
the back of a mountain, or glimpsed
through forest pines, a sun-*rise*? –

and how red the sea is just before
the flat crimson nose slips out
bringing the rest of the orb with it –

but now, when she gets there, the sky
is clouded, and the new sun hidden.
She sits on the sand, watching –

till a crack in the cloud forms
and a slice of the sun is revealed
redder than anything she's seen –

then the whole ball slowly rising
above the red-streaked waves, while
a man from Nürnberg videos it –

with her, motionless, memorising
as the red gradually burns off
leaving a haze that hurts the eyes –

time, then, to speak to the sun,
tell it today's show was a stunner,
as she does, and the video catches it.

EGG

Ask in a beach café for a boiled egg
and it comes raw — well, it's hot
but when your hands grow oven gloves
to prise the shell off in shards
a fissure forms and liquid white
drops out, leaving a clear glimpse
of raw yolk. You call the waiter,
tell him it's *not boiled* — you can't
eat this with a knife & fork! He agrees,
instigates a replacement. It comes,
eventually, and is even hotter,
a real test of the asbestos fingers,
but the shell comes off, with the egg
intact, until the knife attacks it,
meeting — you can't believe it — *soft yolk*
which floods out onto your plate,
with not an egg-spoon in sight.
You do your best to eat it, but run —
a safe hour later — into the sea
and swallow as much of the salty water
as you can — the extra salty water,
one should say, this being the Black Sea.
Egg-taste recurs all day. That evening
you order, in a restaurant, pork stew
with polenta — a safe choice, you think,
till it arrives with a local variant
your lack of the language blocks you from:
a soft fried egg sitting there on top!

THE FISHERMAN

I tried it from the breakwater,
swung my long rod over my head,
tossed my line into the waves,
but all I caught in five hours
was a condom. I blamed the sulphur
seeping from the earth there,
tainting the air and possibly the sea.
I went to the next breakwater,
joined the jostle of anglers.
All, except me, hooked a fish.
So I took my rod to the port
in Mangalia, walked the pier,
set up by the old lighthouse
above where the trawlers dock.
I saw a perch-pike jump once
but my hook missed it. *My worms*,
I thought, and dumped them,
bought the best prawns instead.
Still no biters at the pier-side,
so next day I hired a boat,
phut-phutted well away from land,
flung my line out and drifted
but the only movement was the swell
as a storm got up, making me
scarper for shore and barely make it.
I decided I was done with the Black Sea
or it had done for me. Maybe
one needed to be local, so I retreated
inland a handful of metres,
took my position among the men
who haunt the lakeside there.
For sure, it felt like a demotion –
saltwater for fresh – but I learned
the art of horizontal rodding,
and how a small seat is useful,

and a plastic bag in the water
keeps the caught fish alive,
and how essential it is to start early –
and, of course, the stupendous sense
of having multiple rods, all
sticking out in parallel. Today,
for example, I have four, and still
I've caught nothing, but the line on one
shook twice, and tomorrow I'll arrive
at 6, with eight rods, all of them red,
and a giant plastic bag for the fish.

STONE

for Sandra

The stone angel is yawning,
the stone angel is blowing kisses.
I want to throw an orange.
I want to throw all the oranges
at you, sitting in the leather chair,
at you, sitting curled up on the sofa.
The cat is drinking from the pool,
the cat is going into the pool.
I will fling it in myself.
I will fling myself in after it.
The rooster won't stop crowing.
The rooster won't chase a hen.
The stone angel knows all this.
The stone angel sits up high.
I want to be made of stone.
I want to shout slogans
at you, about Antarctic cruises,
at you, about English red wine.
The cat is stealing a slice of ham.
The cat is going to get very wet.
I will dry it with a towel.
I will stroke it till it purrs.
The rooster is quiet at last.
The rooster has turned to stone.

BLACK MOON

For white he used toothpaste,
for red, blood – but only his own
that he hijacked just enough of each day.

For green he crushed basil in a little
olive oil. His yellow was egg yolk,
his black, coal dust dampened with water.

He tried several routes to blue
before stopping at the intersection
of bilberry juice and pounded bluebells.

His brown was his own, too, applied
last thing in the day before the first
Laphroaig, and the stone jug of ale.

He used no other colours, but his tone
was praised by Prince Haisal, no less,
which got him a rake of commissions

and a residency-offer in Kuwait
which he turned down. At home
the Royal Family was less generous

so he painted them all, in a series
that came to be called his brown period,
though this was strictly incorrect.

He never exhibited with other painters,
never drank with them, spoke of them –
never even spat at their work.

A cave in the Orkneys was his last dwelling
and he rode a horse to his studio.
There were no people in these paintings,

which were found piled up on one another
inside the cave, with no sign of him,
and on top was a depiction of a black moon.

BEFORE THE PERFORMANCE

The elephants are stomping overhead,
the crocodiles are waiting in the rain,
the tigers are sleeping on the stairs,
the lion will arrive here very soon,
the monkeys are swinging from the lights,
the vultures throw shadows on the moon,
the baby hippo's wedged in the bath,
the ostrich has kicked out every pane,
the parrots are shrieking out our names,
the leopards have eaten half a man,
the rhino has fallen through the floor,
the toucan is squawking down the phone,
the baboon has broken all the chairs,
the jackals are rooting in the bin,
the porcupine is caught in the curtains,
the giraffe is fed up bending down,
the waterbuck is waiting for the shower,
the cheetah is running all around,
the zebra is zapped before the mirror,
the hyenas have their eyes on everyone.